SOUNDS LIKE READING®

BOOK ONE

The Bug in the Jug Wants a Hug

A SHORT VOWEL SOUNDS BOOK

Brian P. Cleary

illustrations by
Jason Miskimins

Consultant:
Alice M. Maday

Ph.D. in Early Childhood Education with a Focus in Literacy
Assistant Professor, Retired
Department of Curriculum and Instruction
University of Minnesota

Ⓜ Millbrook Press/Minneapolis

to Mrs. Voorhees,
my kindergarten teacher in Mission, Kansas
—B.P.C.

Millbrook Press
A division of Lerner Publishing Group, Inc.
241 First Avenue North
Minneapolis, MN 55401 USA

For reading levels and more information, look up this title at www.lernerbooks.com.

Library of Congress Cataloging-in-Publication Data

Cleary, Brian P., 1959–
    The bug in the jug wants a hug : a short vowel sounds book / by
 Brian P. Cleary ; illustrations by Jason Miskimins ; consultant: Alice M. Maday.
        p.   cm. — (Sounds like reading)
    ISBN 978-0-7613-9503-4 (lib. bdg. : alk. paper)
    ISBN 978-0-7613-5194-8 (EB pdf)
    1. English language—Vowels—Juvenile literature. 2. English language—
 Phonetics—Juvenile literature. 3. Reading—Phonetic method—Juvenile
 literature. I. Miskimins, Jason, ill. II. Maday, Alice M. III. Title.
 PE1157.C54 2009
 428.1'3—dc22   2008012766

Manufactured in the United States of America
5 - 36868 - 1082 - 8/4/2016

Dear Parents and Educators,

As a former adult literacy coach and the father of three children, I know that learning to read isn't always easy. That's why I developed **Sounds Like Reading**®—a series that uses a combination of devices to help children learn to read.

This book is the first in the **Sounds Like Reading**® series. It uses rhyme, repetition, illustration, and phonics to introduce young readers to short vowel sounds.

Starting on page 4, you'll see three rhyming words on each left-hand page. These words are part of the sentence on the facing page. They all feature short vowels. As the book progresses, the sentences become more challenging. These sentences contain a "discovery" word—an extra rhyming word in addition to those that appear on the left. Toward the end of the book, the sentences contain two discovery words. Children will delight in the increased confidence that finding and decoding these words will bring. They'll also enjoy looking for the mouse that appears throughout the book. The mouse asks readers to look for words that sound alike.

The bridge to literacy is one of the most important we will ever cross. It is my hope that the **Sounds Like Reading**® series will help young readers to hop, gallop, and skip from one side to the other!

Sincerely,

Brian P. Cleary

Brian P. Cleary

Look for me to help you find the words that sound alike!

Pam

jam

ham

Pam had some **jam** on her **ham**.

bun

fun

sun

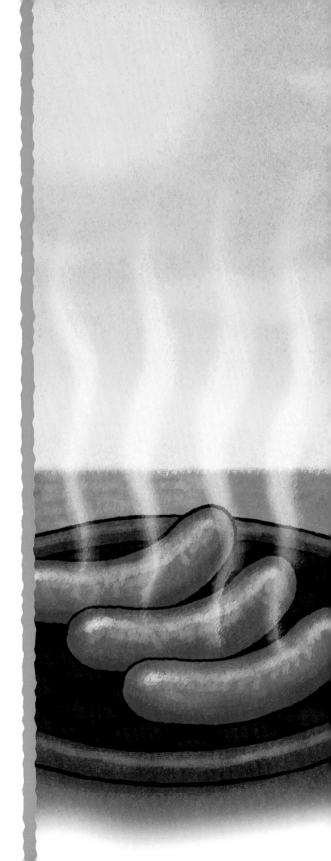

The **bun** had **fun** in the **sun**.

kid

rid

lid

Can you find three words that sound alike?

The **kid** got **rid** of the **lid**.

hen

den

pen

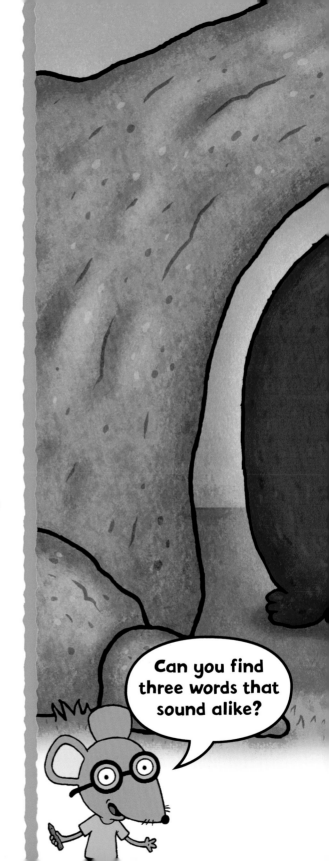

Can you find three words that sound alike?

The **hen** in the **den** has a **pen**.

Dot

hot

cot

Can you find the word that sounds like Dot, hot, and cot?

Dot got hot on the **cot**.

hog

log

dog

Can you find the word that sounds like hog, log, and dog?

A **hog** on a **log** by a **dog** wants to **jog**.

vet

pet

wet

Can you find the word that sounds like vet, pet, and wet?

The **vet** will **get** the **pet wet**.

cat

fat

rat

Can you find the word that sounds like fat, cat, and rat?

A **fat cat sat** on a **rat**.

Ed

bed

red

Ed is **fed** on a **red bed**.

pig

wig

dig

Can you find the word that sounds like pig, wig, and dig?

A **pig** in a **big wig** will **dig**.

mink

ink

sink

Can you find the word that sounds like mink, ink, and sink?

A **pink mink** with **ink** is at the **sink**.

man

can

pan

Can you find two words that sound like man, can, and pan?

The **tan man ran** with a **can** and a **pan.**

Nell

bell

well

Can you find two words that sound like Nell, bell, and well?

Tell Nell that her **bell fell** in the **well**.

bug

jug

rug

A **bug** in a **jug** on a **rug**
by a **mug** wants a **hug**.

Brian P. Cleary is the author of the best-selling Words Are CATegorical® series as well as the Math Is CATegorical® and Adventures in Memory™ series. He has also written several picture books and poetry books. In addition to his work as a children's author and humorist, Mr. Cleary has been a tutor in an adult literacy program. He lives in Cleveland, Ohio.

Jason Miskimins grew up in Cincinnati, Ohio, and graduated from the Columbus College of Art & Design in 2003. He currently lives in North Olmsted, Ohio, where he works as an illustrator of books and greeting cards.

Alice M. Maday has a master's degree in early childhood education from Butler University in Indianapolis, Indiana, and a Ph.D. in early childhood education, with a focus in literacy, from the University of Minnesota in Minneapolis. Dr. Maday has taught at the college level as well as in elementary schools and preschools throughout the country. In addition, she has served as an emergent literacy educator for kindergarten and first-grade students in Germany for the U.S. Department of Defense. Her research interests include the kindergarten curriculum, emergent literacy, parent and teacher expectations, and the place of preschool in the reading readiness process.

For even more phonics fun, check out all eight SOUNDS LIKE READING® titles listed on the back of this book!

And find activities, games, and more at www.brianpcleary.com.